THE LAKE ERIE SHORE
Images of Nature

Connie Smith Girard

March Fourth Publishing Company

The Lake Erie Shore: Images of Nature

Copyright © 1995 by Connie Smith Girard
All rights reserved. No part of this book may be reproduced in any form or by any electronic or mechanical means without written permission from the publisher.

ISBN 1-887018-06-9

Library of Congress Catalog Card Number: 95-75945

Book design and layout by Dianne W. Smith

Printed in Hong Kong

Published in the United States by
MARCH FOURTH PUBLISHING COMPANY
P. O. Box 293031
Kettering, Ohio 45429

This book is dedicated to
my husband and best friend, John Girard,
who shares my love of nature
and the Lake Erie shore.

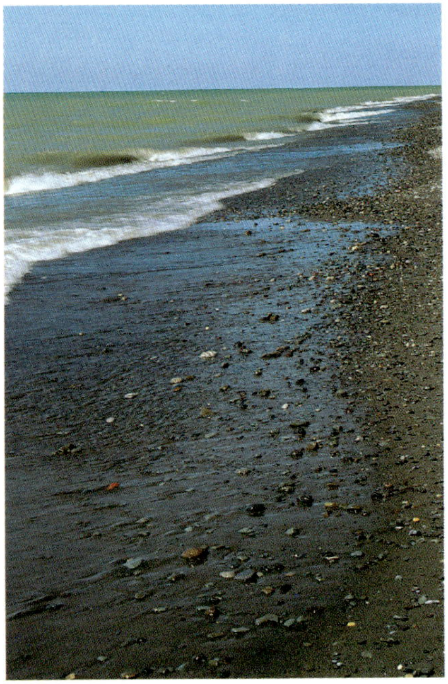

CONTENTS

INTRODUCTION   6

AUTHOR'S NOTES   8

MAP OF LAKE ERIE   10

PART ONE
The Lake Erie Shore   *Michigan and Western Ohio*   13

PART TWO
The Lake Erie Shore   *Eastern Ohio*   37

PART THREE
The Lake Erie Shore   *Pennsylvania and New York*   51

PART FOUR
The Lake Erie Shore   *Ontario*   65

APPENDIX   87

INDEX   91

INTRODUCTION

The Lake Erie Shore: Images of Nature presents a photographic tribute to the natural beauty of the Lake Erie region. This collection of seventy-five color photographs celebrates Lake Erie, one of our country's greatest natural resources. The book takes the reader on a visual journey around the edge of the lake, with stops along the way to look at both sweeping panoramas and detailed close-ups. This pictorial travel and nature guide deliberately focuses on the quiet shore and the diverse environments surrounding the 870-mile perimeter of Lake Erie. The photographs are designed to create a sense of place — to evoke the feel of cool lake breezes and warm sun, the sound of waves lapping on the shore and birds flying overhead, the sight of unlimited blue water and sky, and the calm of the long level horizon line.

The Lake Erie Shore: Images of Nature includes photographs of Lake Erie and surrounding beaches, marshes, forests, fields, and flowers, taken in or near six national parks and reserves, fourteen state or provincial parks, five state nature preserves, and five municipal parks.

Included are images of the lakeshore area and of significant adjacent natural habitats, located up to four miles inland, which represent transition zones that are an integral part of the shoreline environment. These parks and preserves are open to the public for activities such as walking, hiking, photography, art and nature studies, birdwatching, relaxation, and outdoor-living enjoyed near the water's edge. This book is arranged in four chapters or geographic regions which form a loop around Lake Erie. The starting point is in Michigan, the western-most point of the lake. The sequence continues east-northeast through Ohio, Pennsylvania, and New York. Then, at the Canadian border, the direction turns west-southwest and follows the shore through Ontario. A map and an appendix provide additional information.

The Lake Erie Shore: Images of Nature will appeal to travelers, nature lovers, and all who have an appreciation and affinity for the Great Lakes region and Lake Erie. With photographs that involve, inspire, educate, and entertain, *The Lake Erie Shore: Images of Nature* is an invitation to see what makes Lake Erie a beautiful and special place.

AUTHOR'S NOTES

Lake Erie is a place where memories are made. My own connection with Lake Erie began over forty years ago. During the same year I was born, my grandparents built a home in Michigan overlooking Lake Erie. It was 1951, and for the next eight years my mom, dad, sister, and I visited my grandparents' cozy lakefront home many times. Weekends, holidays, and summer vacations were happily spent there, playing in the front yard next to the lake. The wonders of the lake views — the vast expanse of water, the wide horizon line, the big sky — were imprinted upon me at an early age. I have a history with the lake. It is my personal landscape, filled with nature's artwork, found when I was very young, and not forgotten over the years.

When I was a child, Lake Erie was a constant source of delight and adventure. Our days were full of running, playing, splashing, and exploring, among the trees and flowers, always close to the lake. It was all fresh air and fun! Throughout the seasons, Lake Erie provided a picturesque background for our family activities. A few years later my brother was born, and he joined my sister and me in our childhood excitement about the lake. Soon after he learned to talk, he called Lake Erie "grandpa's swimming pool," as if to say we owned it. As if it was possible that the lake, sky, and shore were all ours. As if the endless blue water, spread out before us as far as we could see, existed just for us. But then again... I think it really did.

It has been said that you never actually leave a place you love. Part of it you take with you, leaving a part of yourself behind. Today, Lake Erie is an ongoing source of enjoyment and inspiration to me. I am attracted to the water's edge, captivated by the space, light, movement, and color. I return to the lake frequently to explore natural areas along the shore, finding relaxation and serenity in the quiet places where land meets water and lake meets sky. This book is my tribute to Lake Erie, a special place, where memories are still being made.

C.S.G.

Map of Lake Erie
and surrounding natural areas

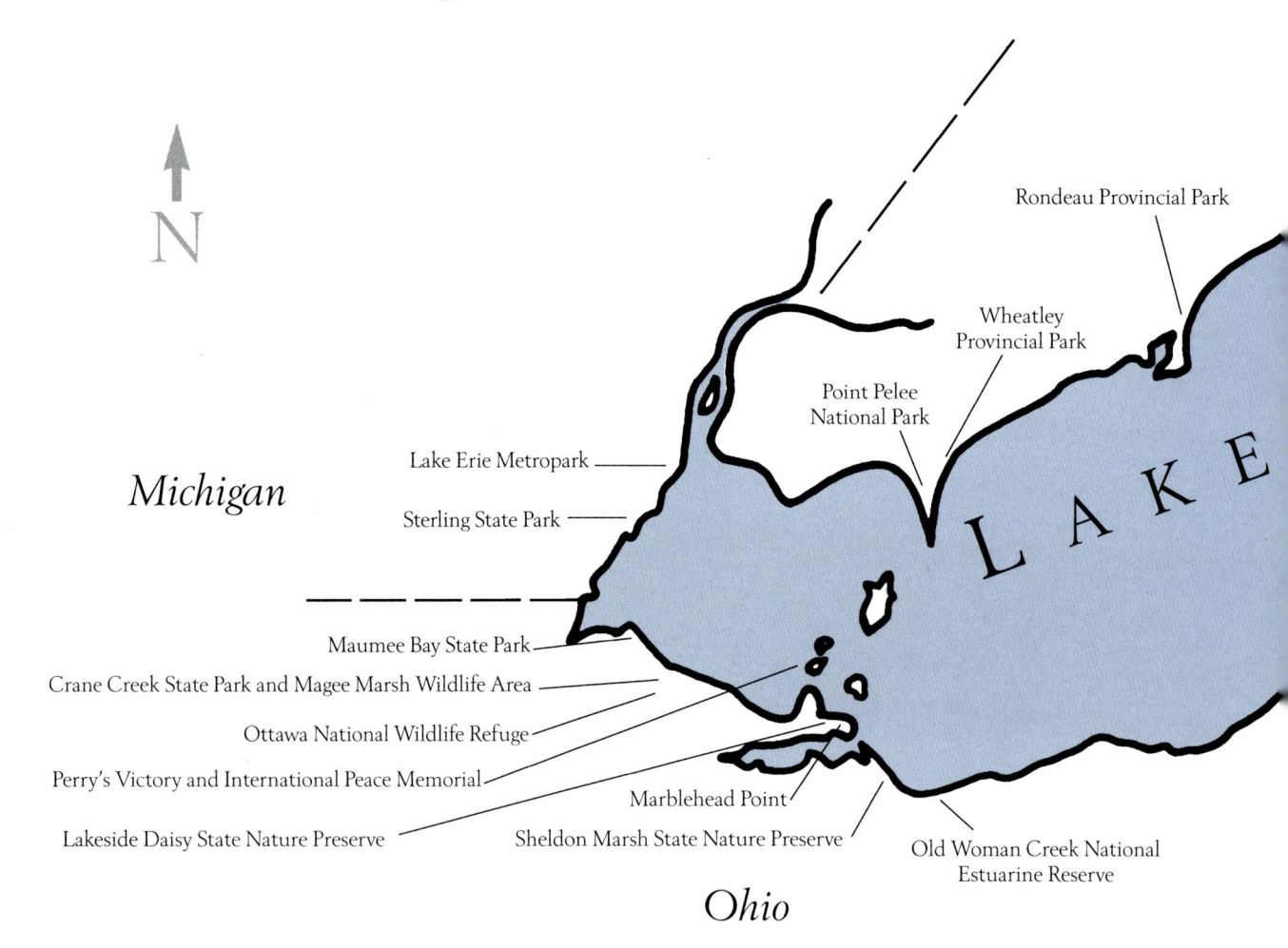

N

Michigan

Ohio

Rondeau Provincial Park
Wheatley Provincial Park
Point Pelee National Park
Lake Erie Metropark
Sterling State Park
Maumee Bay State Park
Crane Creek State Park and Magee Marsh Wildlife Area
Ottawa National Wildlife Refuge
Perry's Victory and International Peace Memorial
Marblehead Point
Lakeside Daisy State Nature Preserve
Sheldon Marsh State Nature Preserve
Old Woman Creek National Estuarine Reserve

LAKE

Ontario

- Rock Point Provincial Park
- Turkey Point Provincial Park
- Long Point Provincial Park
- Niagara Reservation State Park
- Evangola State Park
- Dunkirk Historic Lighthouse
- Lake Erie State Park
- Chautauqua Region

ERIE

New York

Pennsylvania

- Presque Isle State Park
- Geneva State Park
- Lakeshore Reservation Park
- Headlands Beach State Park and Headlands Dunes State Nature Preserve
- Grand River and Paine Falls Park
- Mentor Marsh State Nature Preserve

Sunrise at Lake Erie's western shore, Sterling State Park, Monroe County, Michigan.

LAKE ERIE

PART ONE
Michigan and Western Ohio

Early morning reflections on the lagoon at Sterling State Park.

Mare's tail cloud over Lake Erie Metropark.

First light, Maumee Bay State Park, Lucas County, Ohio.

Monarch butterflies during fall migration, Maumee Bay State Park.

Autumn along Crane Creek, Ottawa National Wildlife Refuge.

Natural beauty and environmental education are offered throughout the
8,000 acres of Ottawa National Wildlife Refuge.

Large varieties of birds are attracted to the Lake Erie region, Crane Creek State Park.

Acres of rose mallow bloom every August at Magee Marsh Wildlife Area.

Gulls on the beach at Crane Creek State Park.

Lake Erie view from atop Marblehead Lighthouse, which was built in 1821, and is the oldest lighthouse in continuous operation on the Great Lakes.

Limestone ledges line the Lake Erie shore at Marblehead Point, Ottawa County, Ohio.

Whitecaps meet the rocky coastline of the Marblehead Peninsula.

Swirling waves at Marblehead Point.

Sunset over Lake Erie, Ottawa County, Ohio.

Lake Erie islands, South Bass, Gibraltar, and Rattlesnake, as seen from the observation deck of Perry's Victory and International Peace Memorial.

Lakeside daisies grow in a limestone quarry at Lakeside Daisy State Nature Preserve on the Marblehead Peninsula.

The rare lakeside daisy, on the federal threatened species list, blooms each May at Lakeside Daisy State Nature Preserve.

Windswept beach with driftwood, Sheldon Marsh State Nature Preserve, Erie County, Ohio.

Lake Erie's unlimited horizon line, Sheldon Marsh State Nature Preserve.

A quiet early spring view of the waterways at Sheldon Marsh State Nature Preserve.

Rose mallow and monarch butterfly, Sheldon Marsh State Nature Preserve.

The butterfly meadow, part of the lake-marsh-forest ecosystem along Lake Erie's western basin at Sheldon Marsh State Nature Preserve.

Migrating Canada geese fly over Sheldon Marsh State Nature Preserve.

Old Woman Creek meets and mixes with Lake Erie, forming a freshwater estuary, Old Woman Creek National Estuarine Reserve and State Nature Preserve.

PART TWO

Eastern Ohio

Nature's mosaic on the barrier beach at Old Woman Creek National Estuarine Reserve, Erie County, Ohio.

One of the first signs of spring at Old Woman Creek National Estuarine Reserve.

Water lotus fills the estuary, Old Woman Creek National Estuarine Reserve.

Beach pea at the environmentally significant Headlands Dunes State Nature Preserve, Lake County, Ohio.

The mile-long expanse of Headlands Beach is Ohio's longest natural beach on Lake Erie. Fairport Harbor and Grand River Lighthouse are in the distance, Headlands Dunes State Nature Preserve.

Sunset through the cottonwoods at Headlands Beach State Park.

Killdeer birdnest in the sand, Headlands Dunes State Nature Preserve.

Plume grass prevails over the National Natural Landmark, Mentor Marsh State Nature Preserve.

Waterfall at Paine Creek, Paine Falls Park.

The Grand River, designated a Wild and Scenic River by the State of Ohio.

The Grand River surrounded by autumn color, Lake County, Ohio.

Pebble beach, Lakeshore Reservation Park.

Tall reed grass at the edge of Lake Erie, Geneva State Park.

Sunlight and shadow on white birch trees at Presque Isle State Park, Erie County, Pennsylvania.

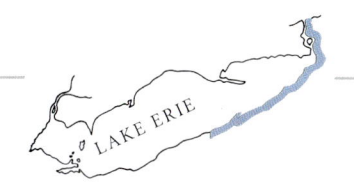

PART THREE
Pennsylvania and New York

Lake Erie forms the background for the 3200-acre, seven-mile peninsula of Presque Isle State Park.

Cattails in winter near Marina Lake, Presque Isle State Park.

Wintertime vineyard. Over 40,000 acres of grapes are produced in the Chautauqua and Erie region near Lake Erie.

Barcelona Harbor and the bluffs of Chautauqua County, New York.

Spruce tree, Chautauqua County, New York.

Shades of autumn color at Chautauqua Creek.

Trees and shrubs line the top of the bluffs overlooking Lake Erie at Lake Erie State Park.

Lake Erie from atop the historic 1875 Dunkirk Lighthouse, Dunkirk Historical Lighthouse Park.

Flowering trees at Lake Erie's edge, Point Gratiot Park.

Bluffs at Silver Creek, Chautauqua County, New York.

Frozen and snow covered Lake Erie, Evangola State Park.

Frost flowers form on the frozen Niagara River at Three Sisters Islands, Niagara Reservation State Park.

The cusp of American Falls at Niagara Falls, Prospect Point, Niagara Reservation State Park, Niagara County, New York.

Rocks clustered along the limestone shelf shoreline of Rock Point Provincial Park, Haldimand-Norfolk Region, Ontario.

LAKE ERIE

PART FOUR
Ontario

Deserted Mohawk Island Lighthouse, Rock Point Provincial Park.

Columbine wildflowers grace Rock Point Provincial Park.

Fruit tree orchard, Haldimand-Norfolk Region, Ontario.

Fall leaves provide brilliant color near Turkey Point Provincial Park.

Sedges, grasses, and trees cover the low ridges and dunes next to Lake Erie at Long Point Provincial Park.

Sand dunes and cottonwood trees line the Lake Erie shore at Long Point Provincial Park.

Long Point peninsula has been designated a unique World Biosphere Reserve by UNESCO/United Nations Educational, Scientific, and Cultural Organization, Long Point Provincial Park.

Rock, sand, and wind formation, Long Point Provincial Park.

Beach grasses at Long Point Provincial Park.

The largest southern hardwood forest in Ontario stands at Rondeau Provincial Park, Kent County, Ontario.

Beach path at Ontario's second oldest park, Rondeau Provincial Park.

Walking along the beach at Rondeau Provincial Park.

Trillium bloom in spring at Wheatley Provincial Park.

Spring wildflowers thrive at Kopegaron Woods Conservation Area.

Welcome to Point Pelee National Park, a unique environment of marsh, forest, field, and beach.

Sea gulls feeding on the sand spit at mainland Canada's southernmost point,
Point Pelee National Park, Essex County, Ontario.

Phlox bloom near Sanctuary Pond, Point Pelee National Park.

Carolinian forest zone along the tip trail at Point Pelee National Park.

Marsh habitat dominates Point Pelee National Park.

The marsh boardwalk reaches into a sea of cattails at Point Pelee National Park.

Sunset at Black Willow Beach on the Lake Erie shore, Point Pelee National Park.

Lake Erie reaches across a 210-mile international border between the United States and Canada, symbolizing nearly two centuries of peace between the two nations.

APPENDIX

INFORMATION SOURCES

Information about the locations included in this book can be obtained from the following sources:

MICHIGAN

Lake Erie Metropark (Wayne County)
32481 West Jefferson
P.O. Box 120
Rockwood, MI 48173
313 379-5020

Sterling State Park (Monroe County)
2800 State Park Road
Route 5
Monroe, MI 48161
313 289-2715

NEW YORK

Chautauqua Allegheny Region (Chautauqua County)
4 North Erie Street
Mayville, NY 14757
800 242-4569

Dunkirk Historical Lighthouse (Chautauqua County)
Lighthouse Point Drive North
Dunkirk, NY 14048

Evangola State Park (Erie County)
Route 5
Irving, NY 14081
716 549-1802

Lake Erie State Park (Chautauqua County)
RD #1
Brocton, NY 14716
716 792-9214

Niagara Reservation State Park (Niagara County)
Prospect Park
P.O. Box 1132
Niagara Falls, NY 14303
716 278-1770

OHIO

Crane Creek State Park (Ottawa County)
1400 Park Road #1
Oregon, OH 43618
419 898-2495

Geneva State Park (Ashtabula County)
P.O. Box 429
Padanarum Road
Geneva, OH 44041
216 466-8400

Headlands Beach State Park (Lake County)
9601 Headlands Road
Mentor, OH 44060
216 257-1330

Headlands Dunes State Nature Preserve (Lake County)
9601 Headlands Road
Mentor, OH 44060
216 563-9344

Lakeshore Reservation Park (Lake County)
Lake Metroparks
8800 Chardon Road
Kirtland, OH 44094
216 256-PARK

Magee Marsh Wildlife Area (Ottawa County)
13229 West State Route 2
Oak Harbor, OH 43449

Marblehead Point (Ottawa County)
Marblehead Peninsula Chamber of Commerce
P.O. Box 268
Marblehead, OH 43440
419 798-9777

Maumee Bay State Park (Lucas County)
1400 Park Road #1
Oregon, OH 43618
419 836-7758

Mentor Marsh State Nature Preserve (Lake County)
5185 Corduroy Road
Mentor, OH 44060
216 257-0777

Old Woman Creek National Estuarine Reserve and State Nature Preserve (Erie County)
2514 Cleveland Road East
Huron, OH 44839
419 433-4601

Ottawa National Wildlife Refuge (Ottawa County)
14000 West State Route 2
Oak Harbor, OH 43449
419 898-0014

Paine Falls Park (Lake County)
Lake Metroparks
8800 Chardon Road
Kirtland, OH 44094
216 256-PARK

Perry's Victory and International Peace Memorial (Ottawa County)
U.S. Department of Interior
National Park Service
P.O. Box 549
Put-in-Bay, OH 43456

Sheldon Marsh State Nature Preserve (Erie County)
2715 Cleveland Road West
Huron, OH 44839
419 433-4919

ONTARIO

Long Point Provincial Park (Haldimand-Norfolk Region)
P.O. Box 99
Port Rowan, Ontario N0E 1M0
519 586-2133

Point Pelee National Park (Essex County)
RR #1
Leamington, Ontario N8H 3V4
519 322-2365

Rock Point Provincial Park (Haldimand-Norfolk Region)
P.O. Box 158
Dunnville, Ontario N1A 2X5
416 774-6642

Rondeau Provincial Park (Kent County)
R.R. 1
Morpeth, Ontario   N0P 1X0
519 674-5405

Turkey Point Provincial Park (Haldimand-Norfolk Region)
Turkey Point, Ontario   N0E 1T0
519 426-3239

Wheatley Provincial Park (Kent County)
P.O. Box 640
Wheatley, Ontario   N0P 2P0
519 825-4659

PENNSYLVANIA

Presque Isle State Park (Erie County)
Department of Environmental Resources
P.O. Box 8510
Erie, PA   16505
814 871-4251

Additional information can be obtained from the following sources:

Michigan State Parks
Department of Natural Resources
Parks and Recreation Division
Box 30257
Lansing, MI   48909
517 373-9900

State of New York
Office of Parks, Recreation and Historic Preservation
Empire State Plaza, Agency Building One
Albany, NY   12238
518 474-0456

Ohio Department of Natural Resources
Division of Parks and Recreation
1952 Belcher Drive
Columbus, OH   43224
614 265-6608

Ohio Department of Natural Resources
Division of Natural Areas and Preserves
1889 Fountain Square, Building F1
Columbus, OH   43224
614 265-6453

State of Pennsylvania
Bureau of State Parks
P.O. Box 8551
Harrisburg, PA   17105
800 63PARKS

Ministry of Natural Resources
Information Center
Room M1-73, Macdonald Block
900 Bay Street
Toronto, Ontario, Canada   M7A 2C1
416 314-2000

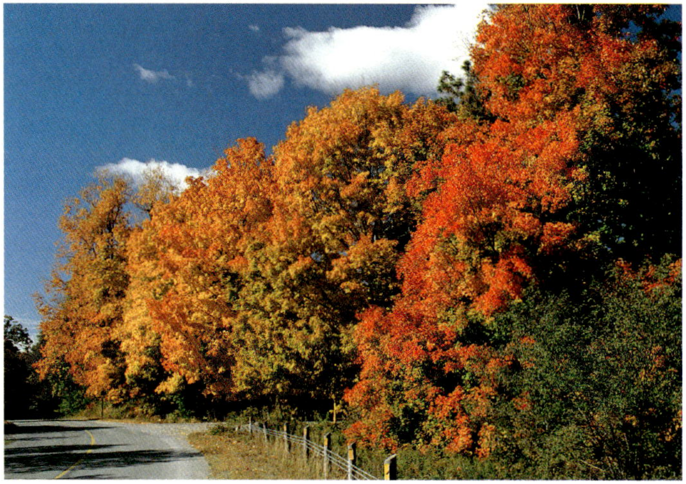

INDEX

Photographs taken in or near these locations can be found on the following pages:

MICHIGAN

Lake Erie Metropark, 14
Sterling State Park, 12, 13

NEW YORK

Chautauqua County, 54 - 56
Dunkirk Historical Lighthouse, 58, 59
Evangola State Park, 60, 61
Lake Erie State Park, 57
Niagara Reservation State Park, 62, 63, 86

OHIO

Crane Creek State Park, 19, 21
Geneva State Park, 49
Grand River, 46, 47
Headlands Beach State Park, 42
Headlands Dunes State Nature Preserve, 40, 41, 43
Lakeshore Reservation Park, 48
Lakeside Daisy State Nature Preserve, 28, 29
Magee Marsh Wildlife Area, 20
Marblehead Point, 22 - 26
Maumee Bay State Park, 15, 16
Mentor Marsh State Nature Preserve, 44
Old Woman Creek National Estuarine Reserve, 36 - 39
Ottawa National Wildlife Refuge, 17, 18
Paine Falls Park, 45
Perry's Victory and International Peace Memorial, 27
Sheldon Marsh State Nature Preserve, 30 - 35

ONTARIO

Long Point Provincial Park, 69 - 73
Point Pelee National Park, 79 - 85
Rock Point Provincial Park, 64 - 66
Rondeau Provincial Park, 74 - 76
Turkey Point Provincial Park, 67, 68
Wheatley Provincial Park, 77, 78

PENNSYLVANIA

Presque Isle State Park, 50 - 53

ORDER INFORMATION

____ The Lake Erie Shore: *Images of Nature* $25.00 each _____

Shipping $2.50 each _____

Sales Tax 6.5% on Ohio residents' orders $1.63 each _____

TOTAL ORDER $ _____

☐ Check

☐ Visa_____
CREDIT CARD NUMBER

☐ MasterCard_____
CREDIT CARD NUMBER

_____
EXPIRATION DATE

_____
SIGNATURE

NAME_____

ADDRESS_____

CITY_____ STATE_____ ZIP_____

Send order form and payment to:

March Fourth Publishing Company
P.O. Box 293031
Kettering, OH 45429

(Order form may be copied)
Thank You